ZOMBIES
Going Walkies

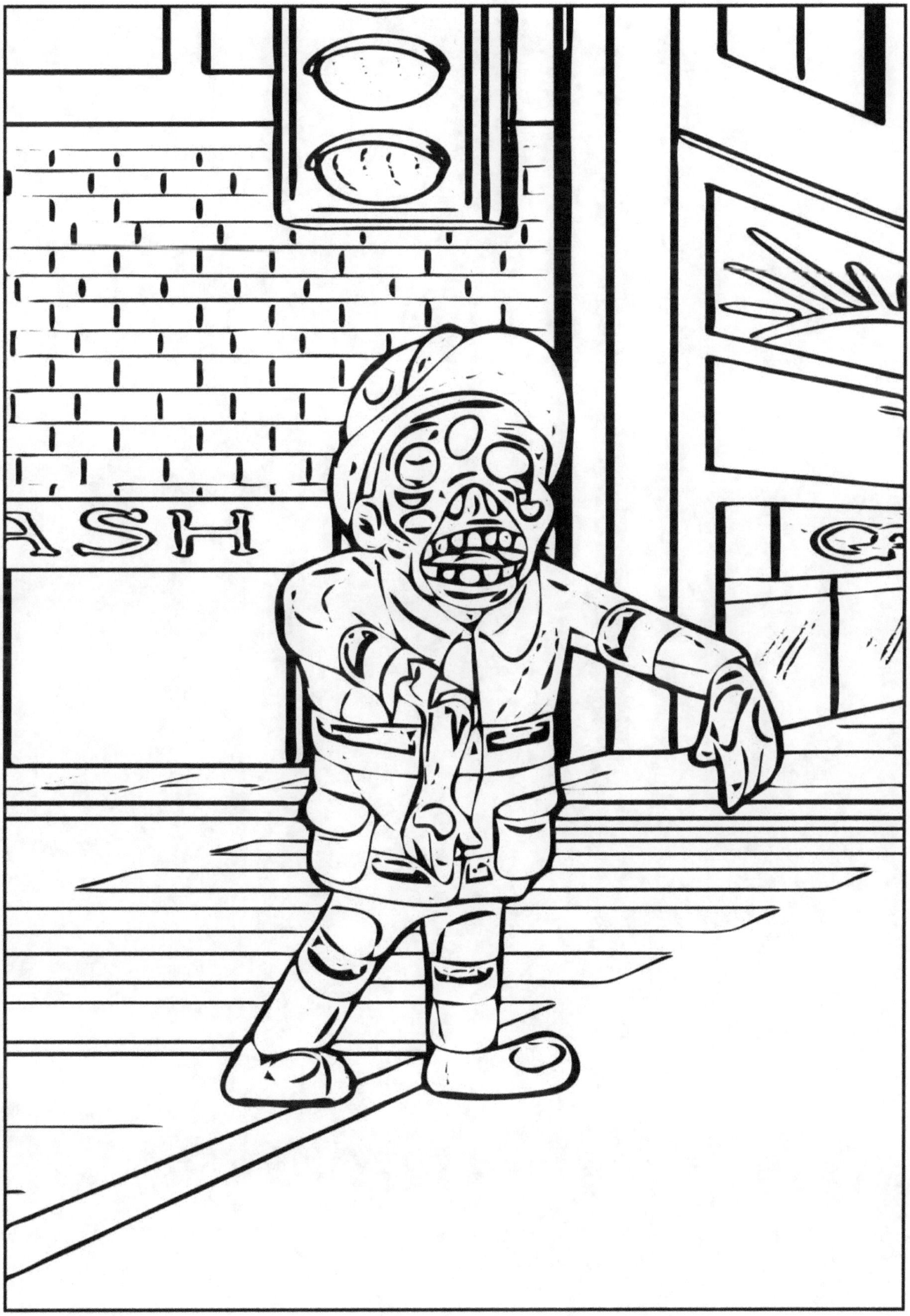
ASH

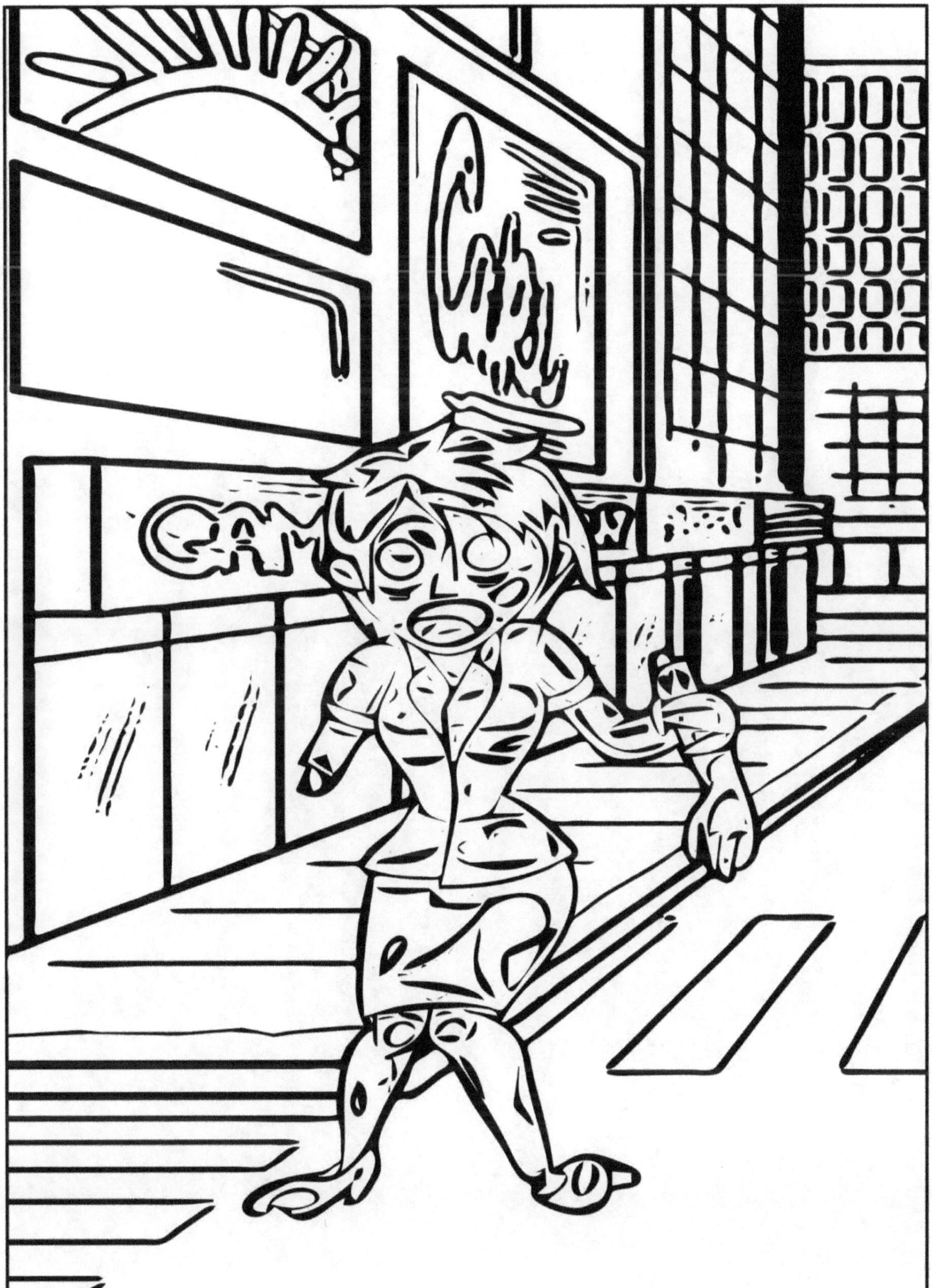

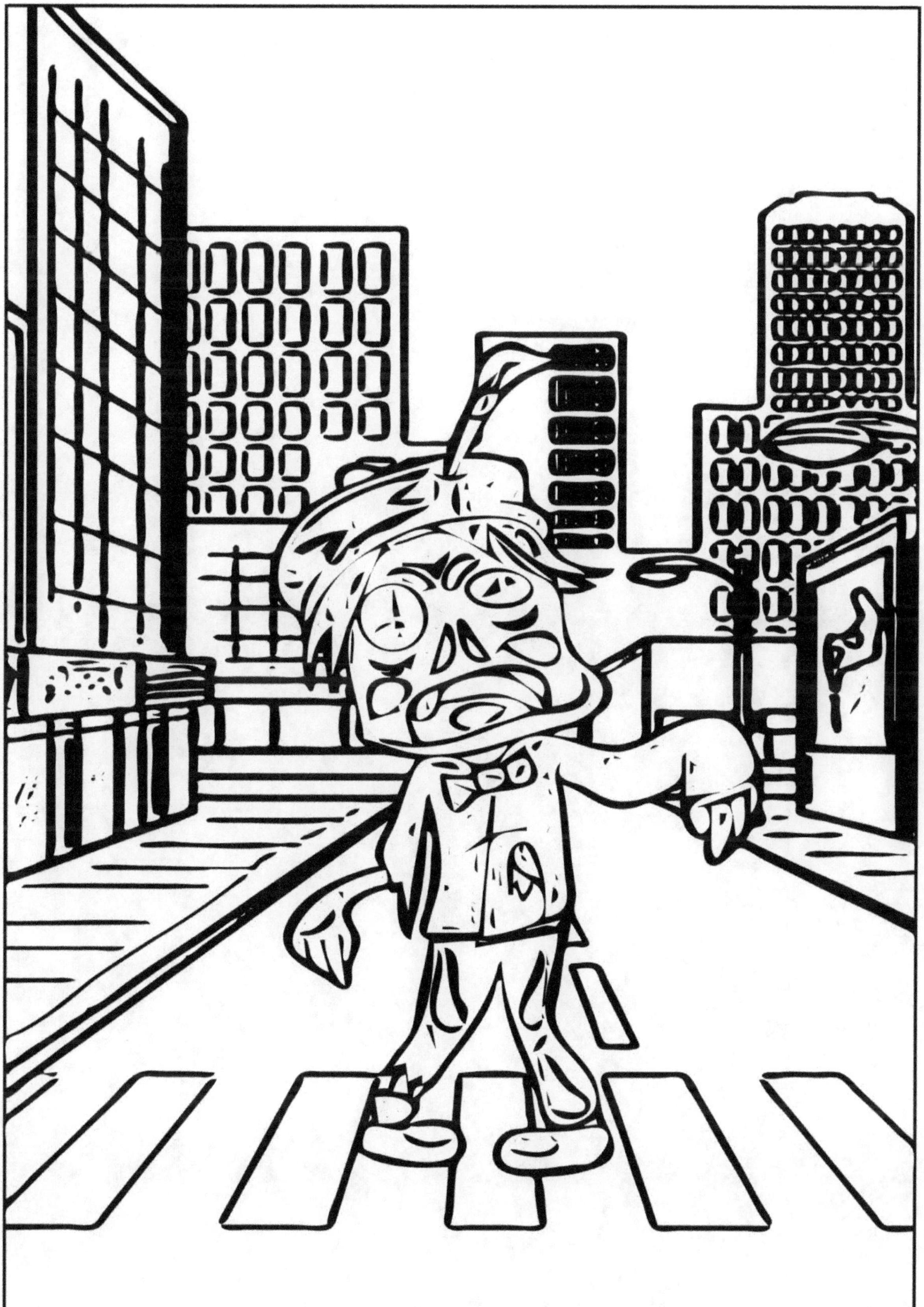

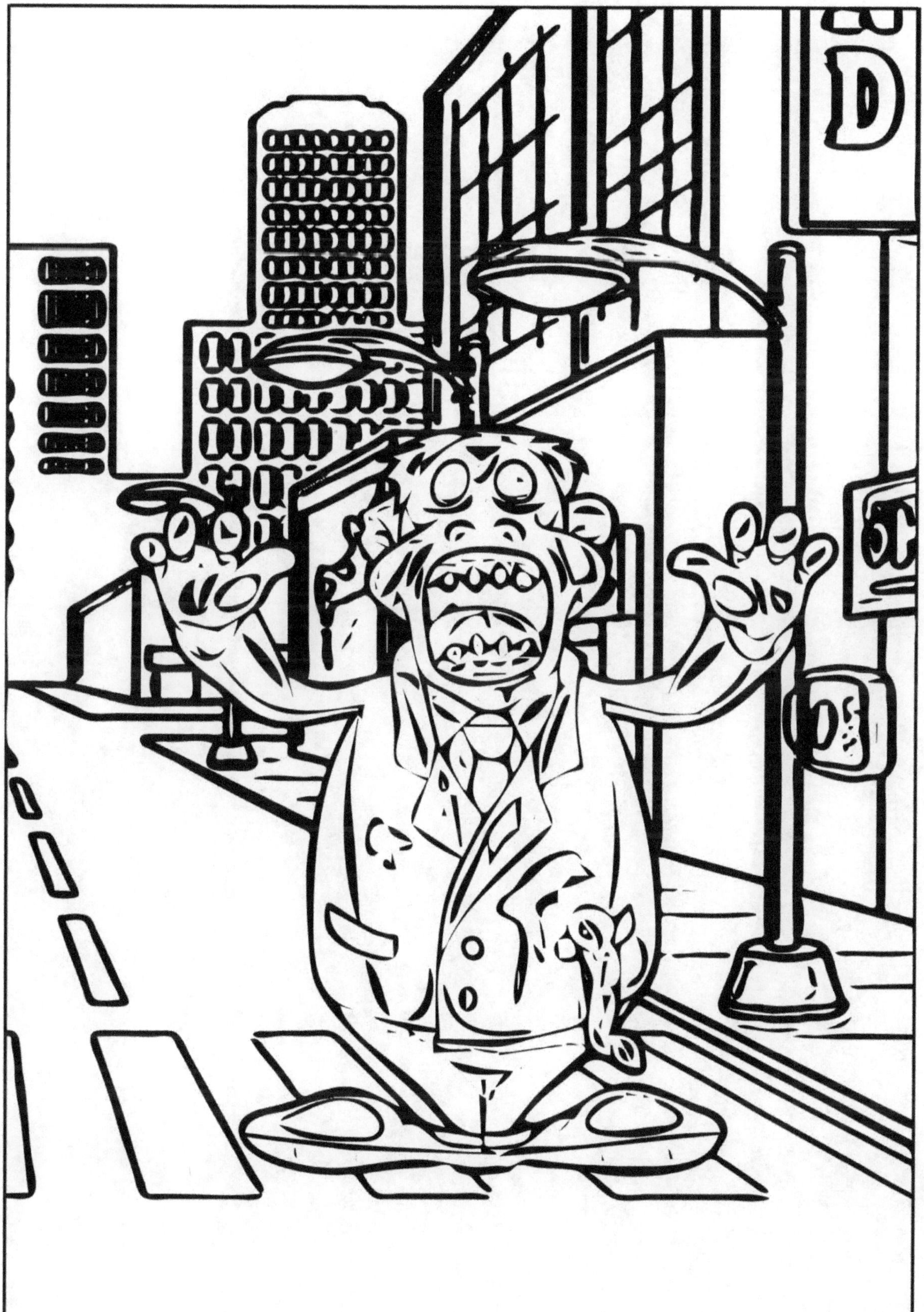

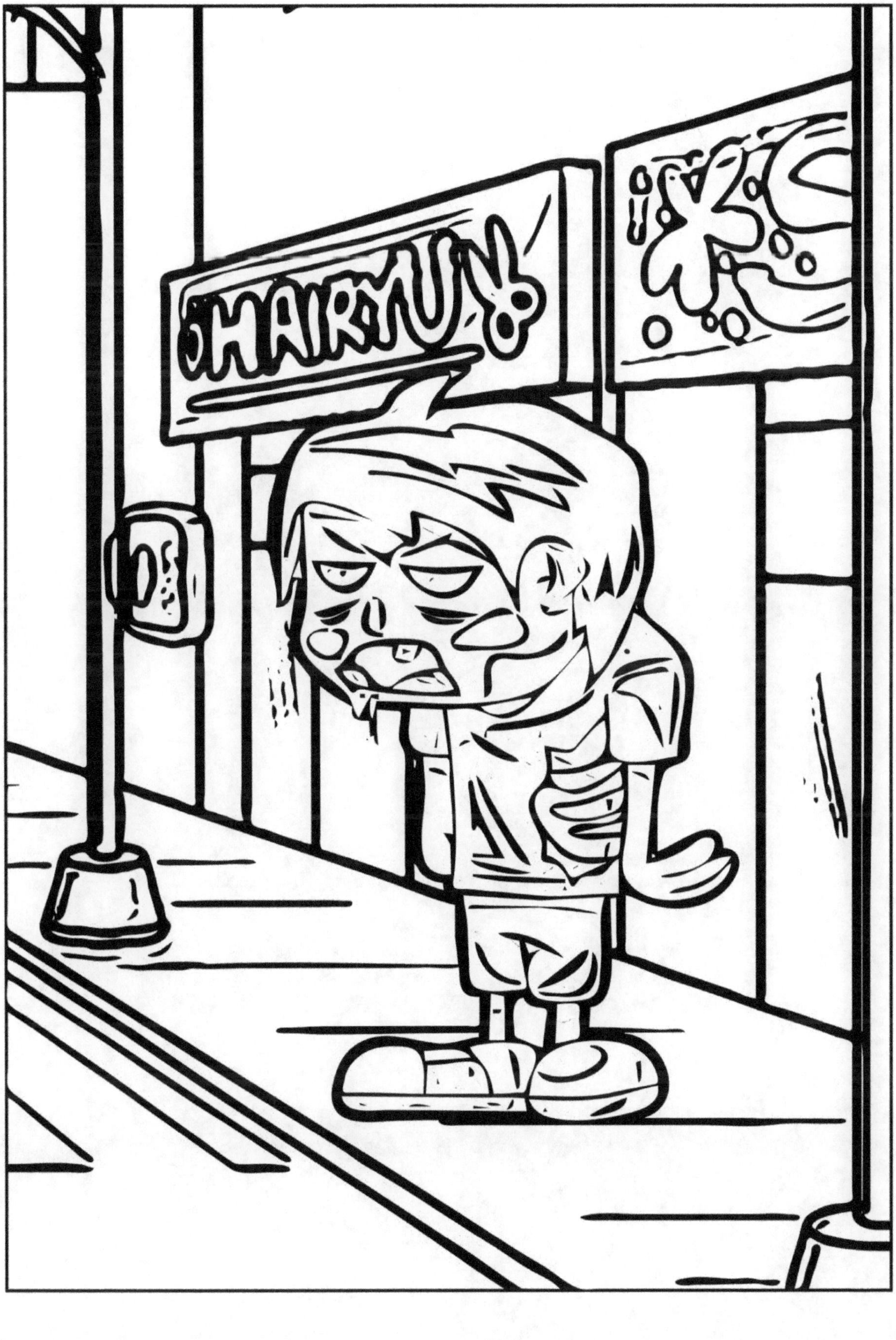

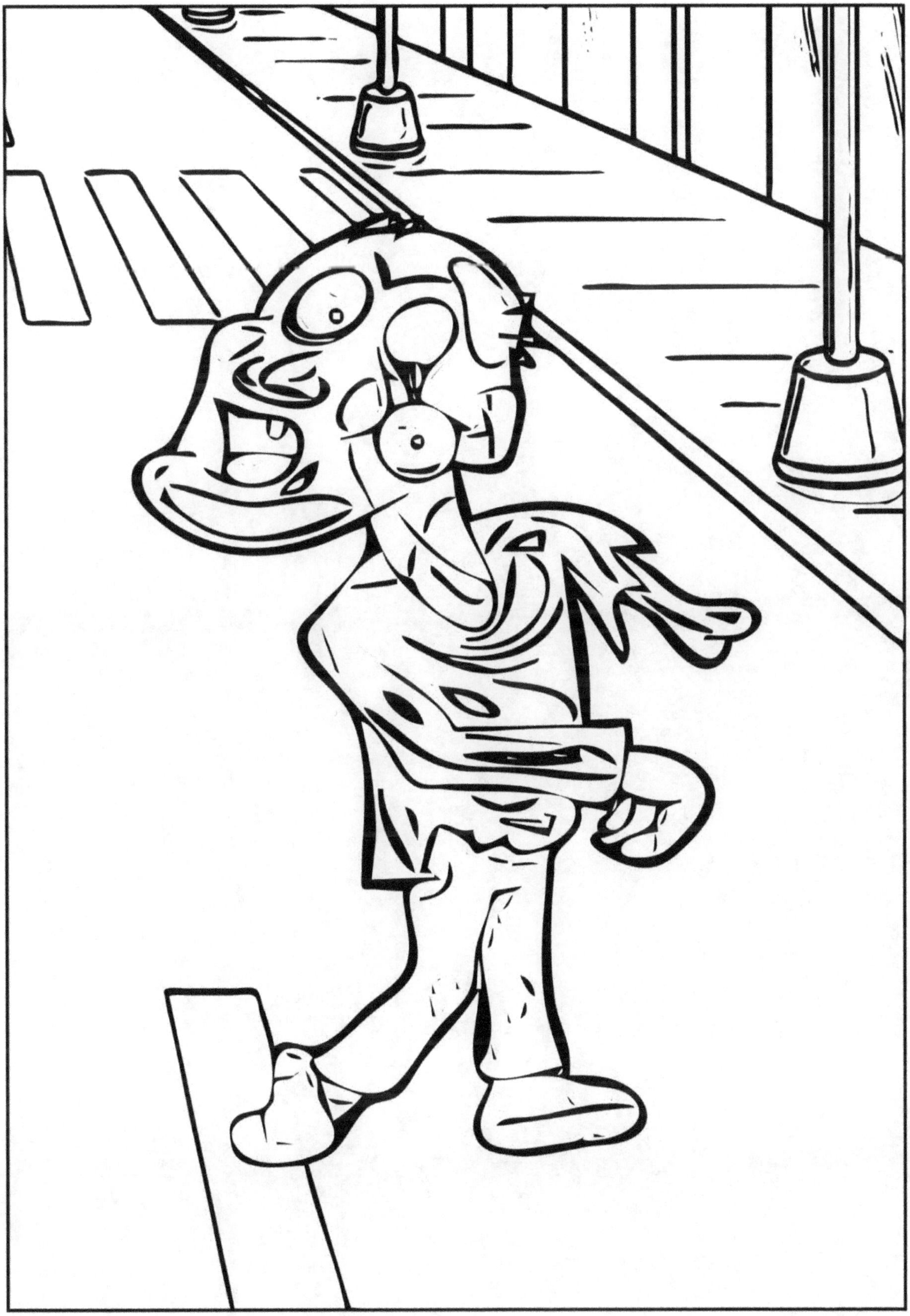

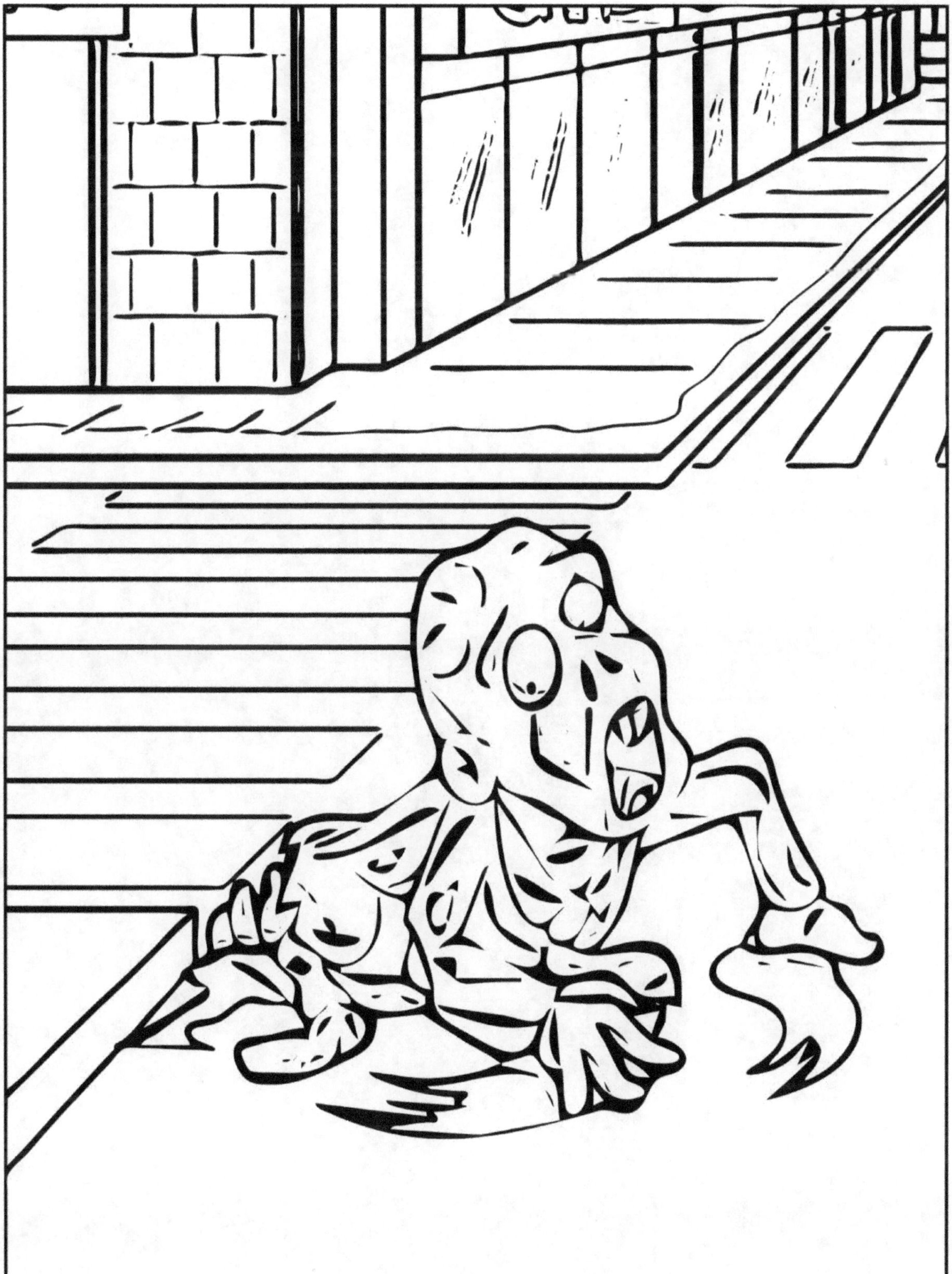

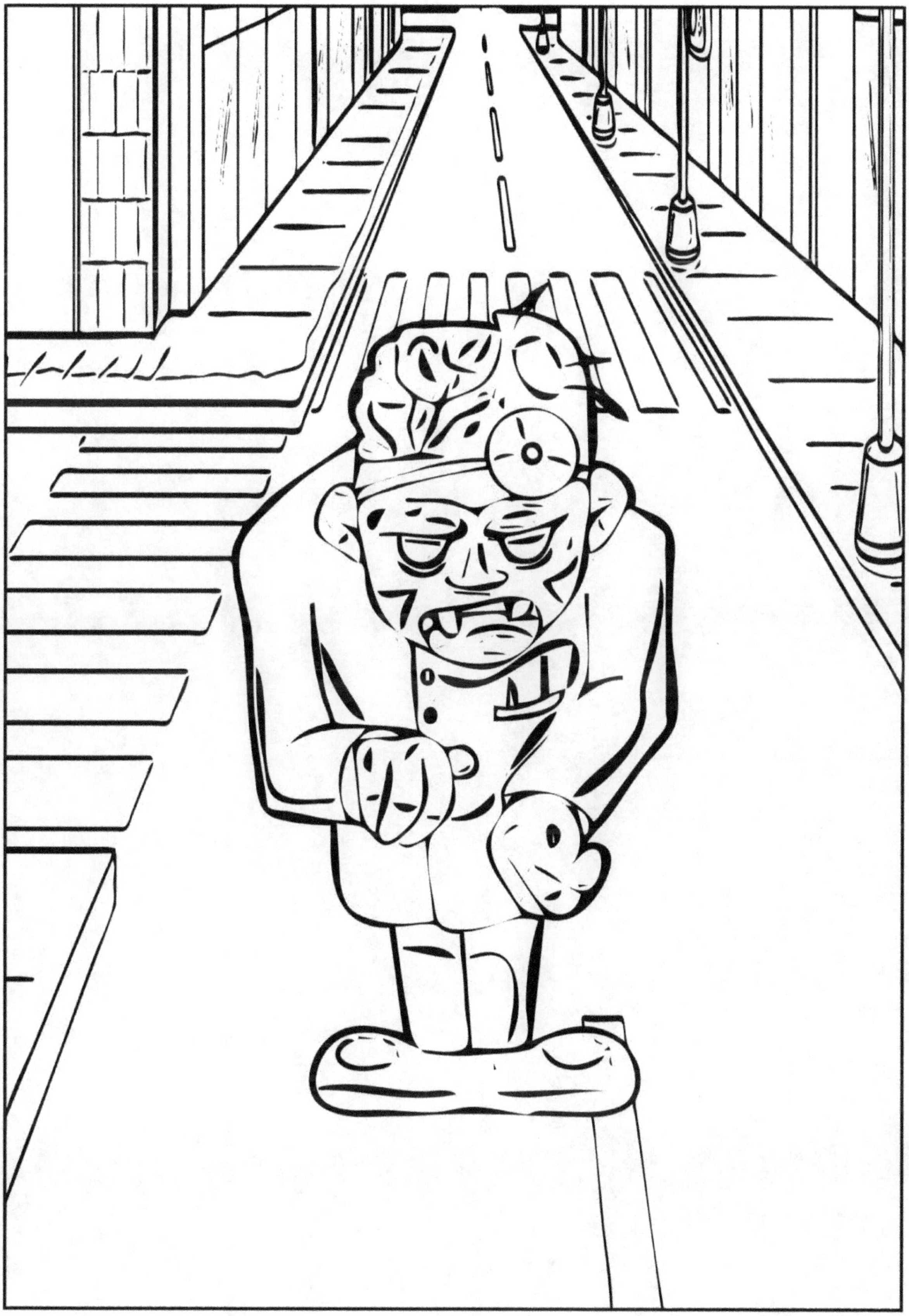

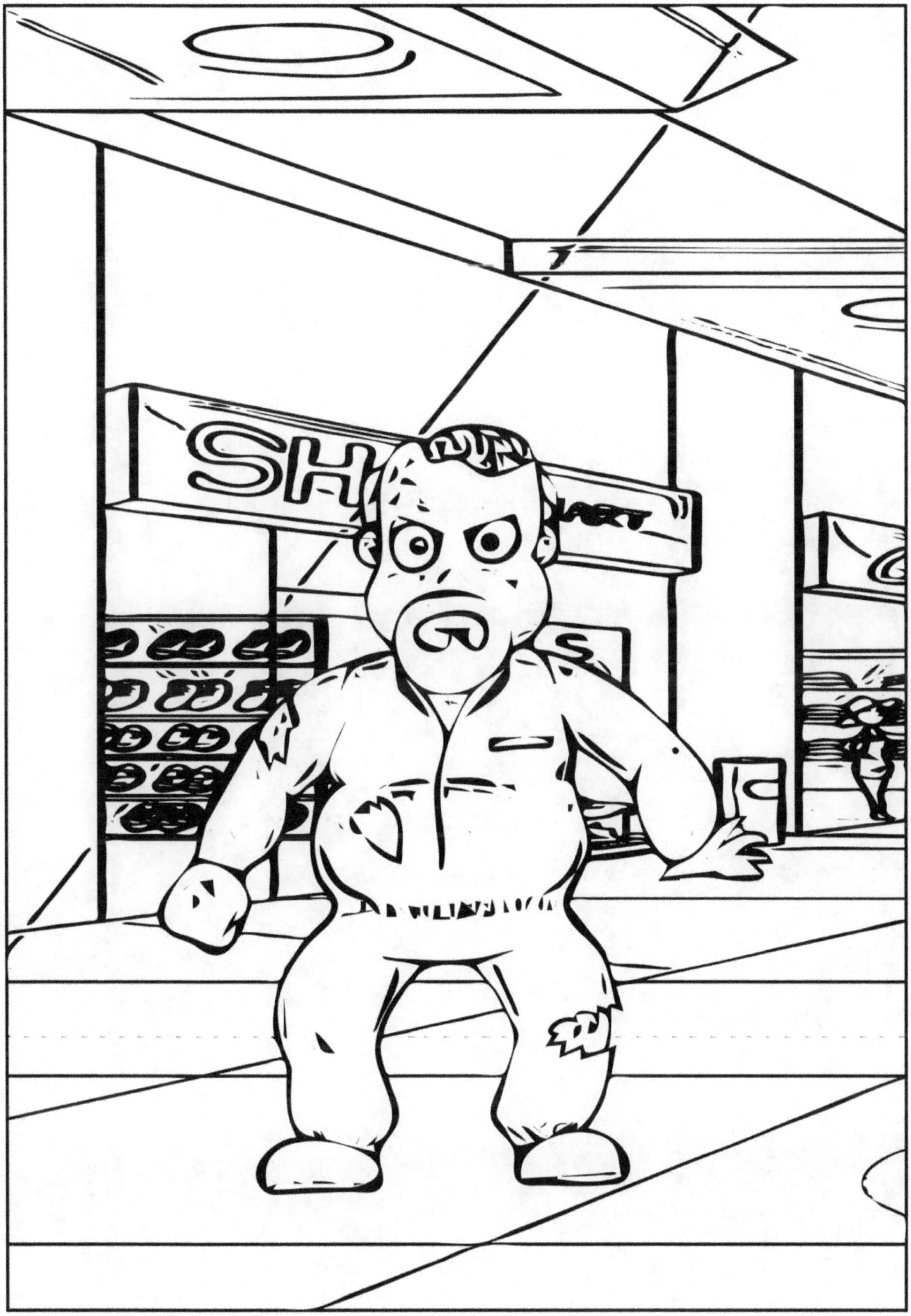
SH

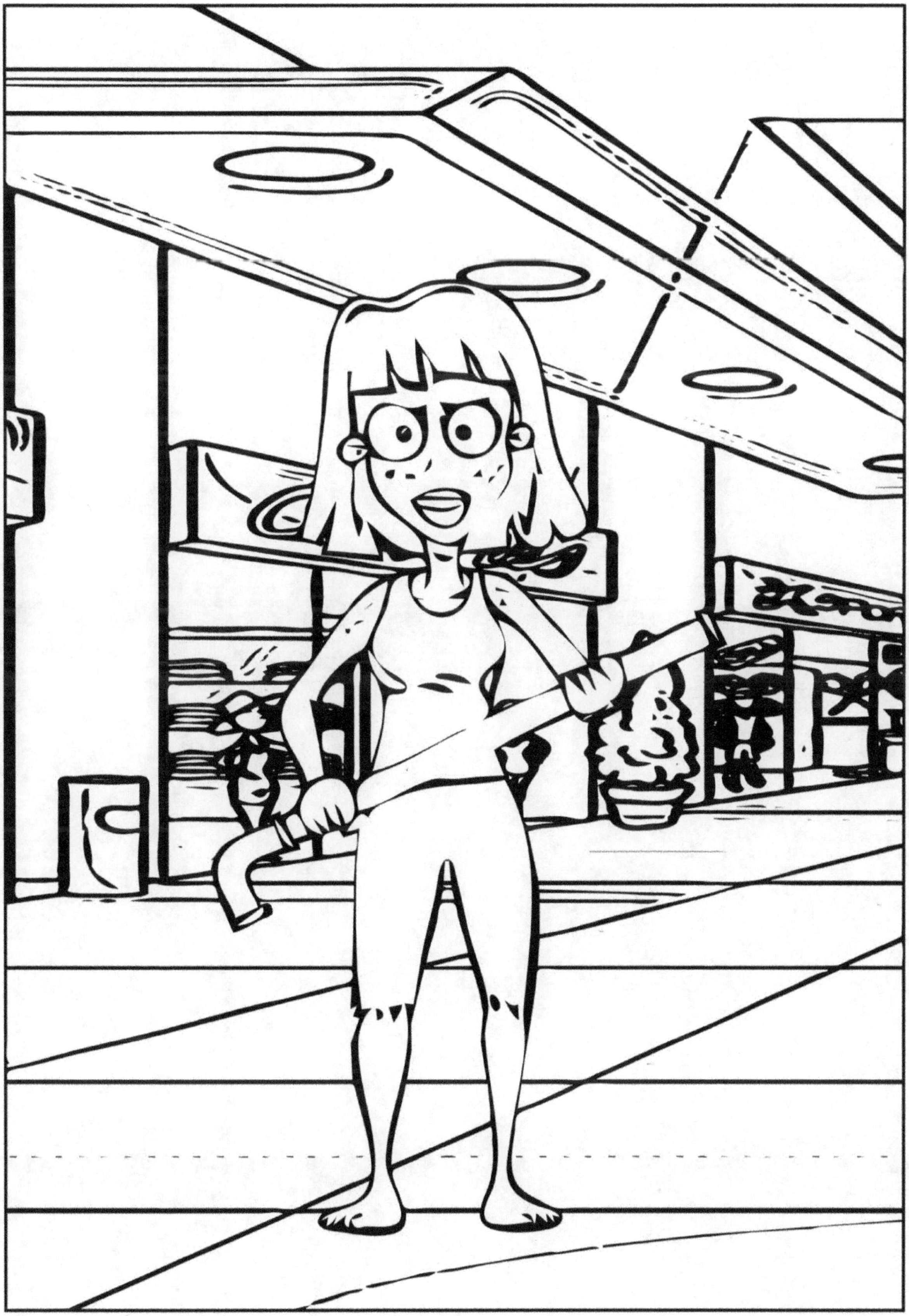

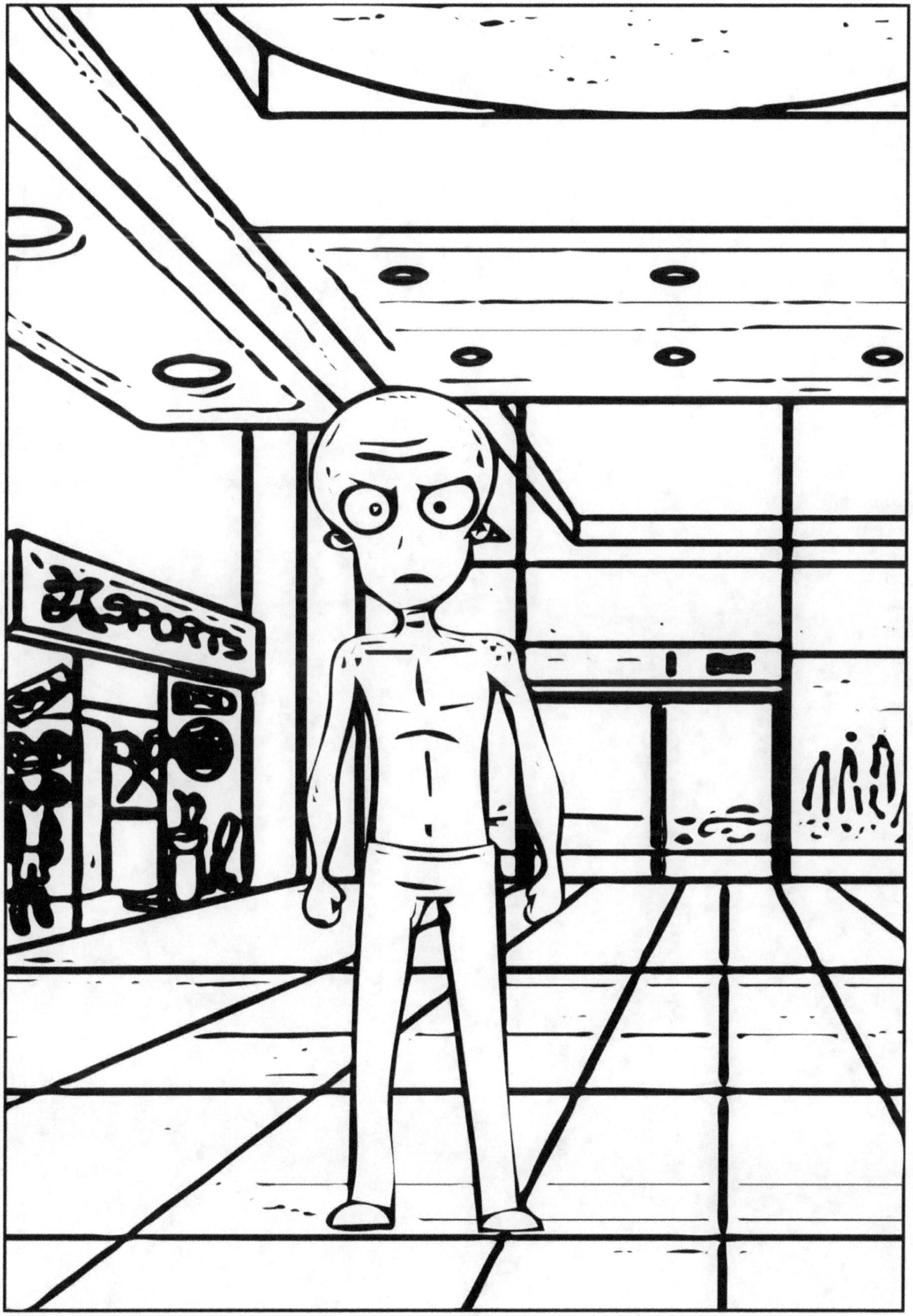
SPORTS

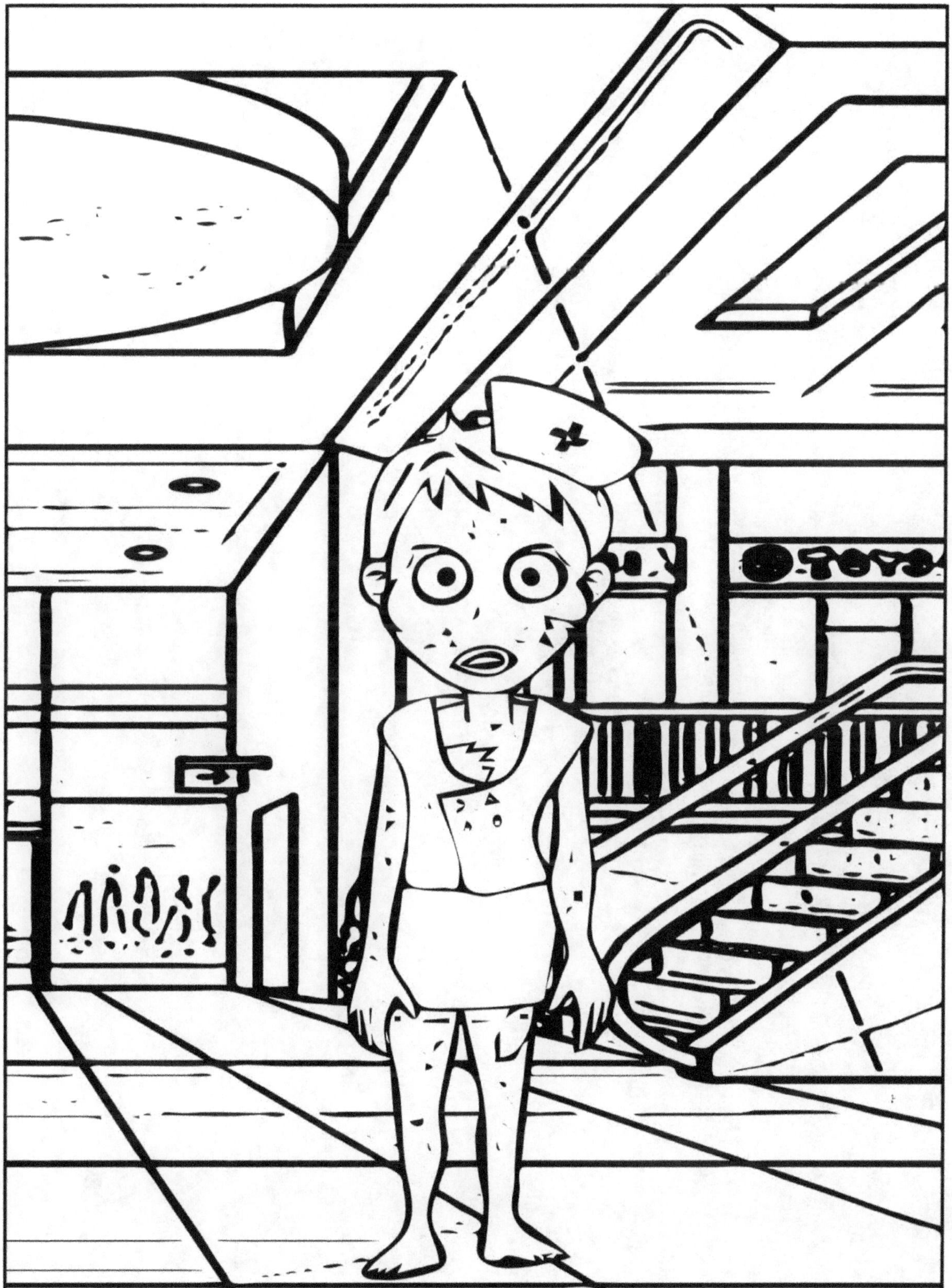
TOYS

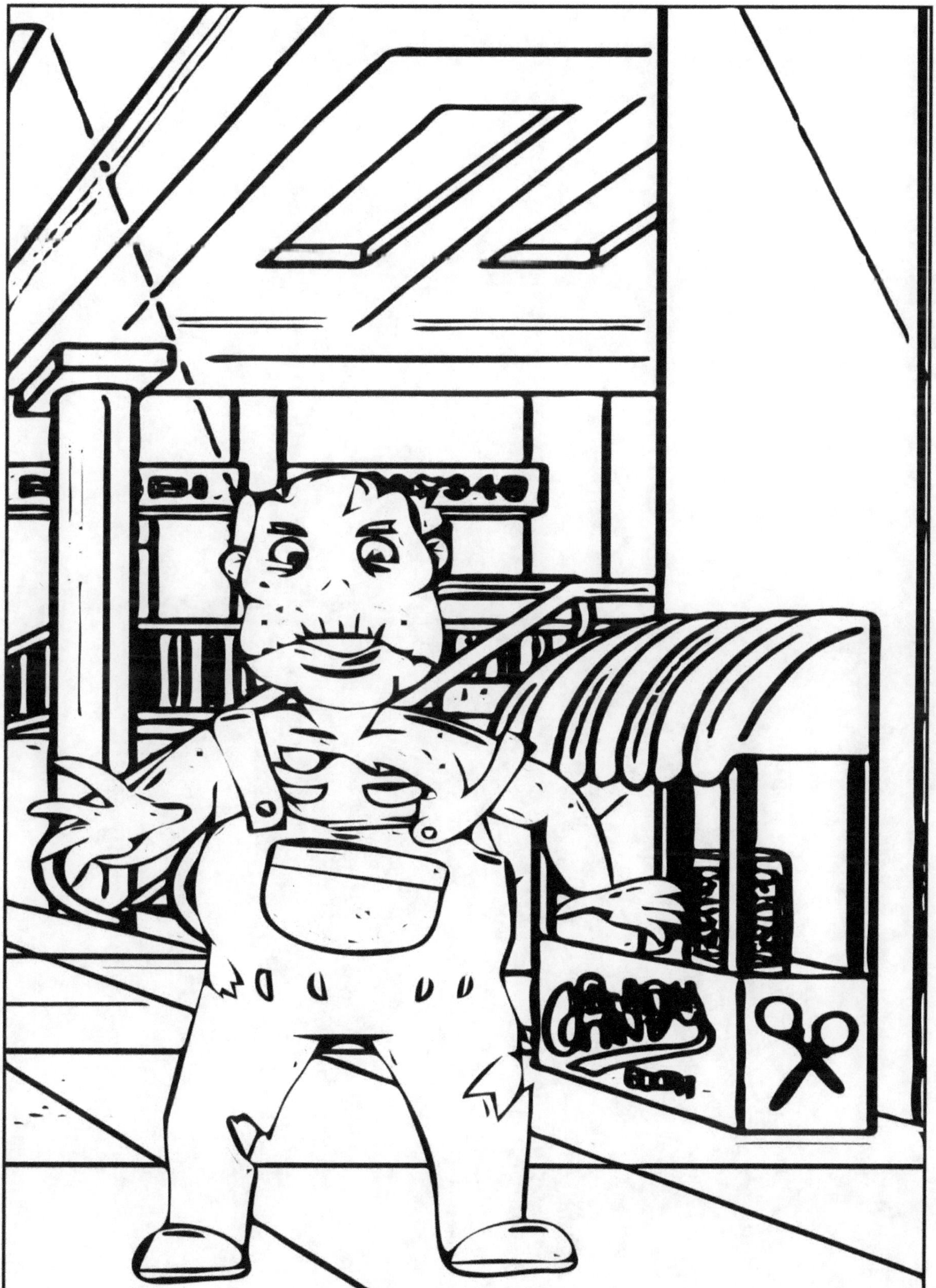
CANDY

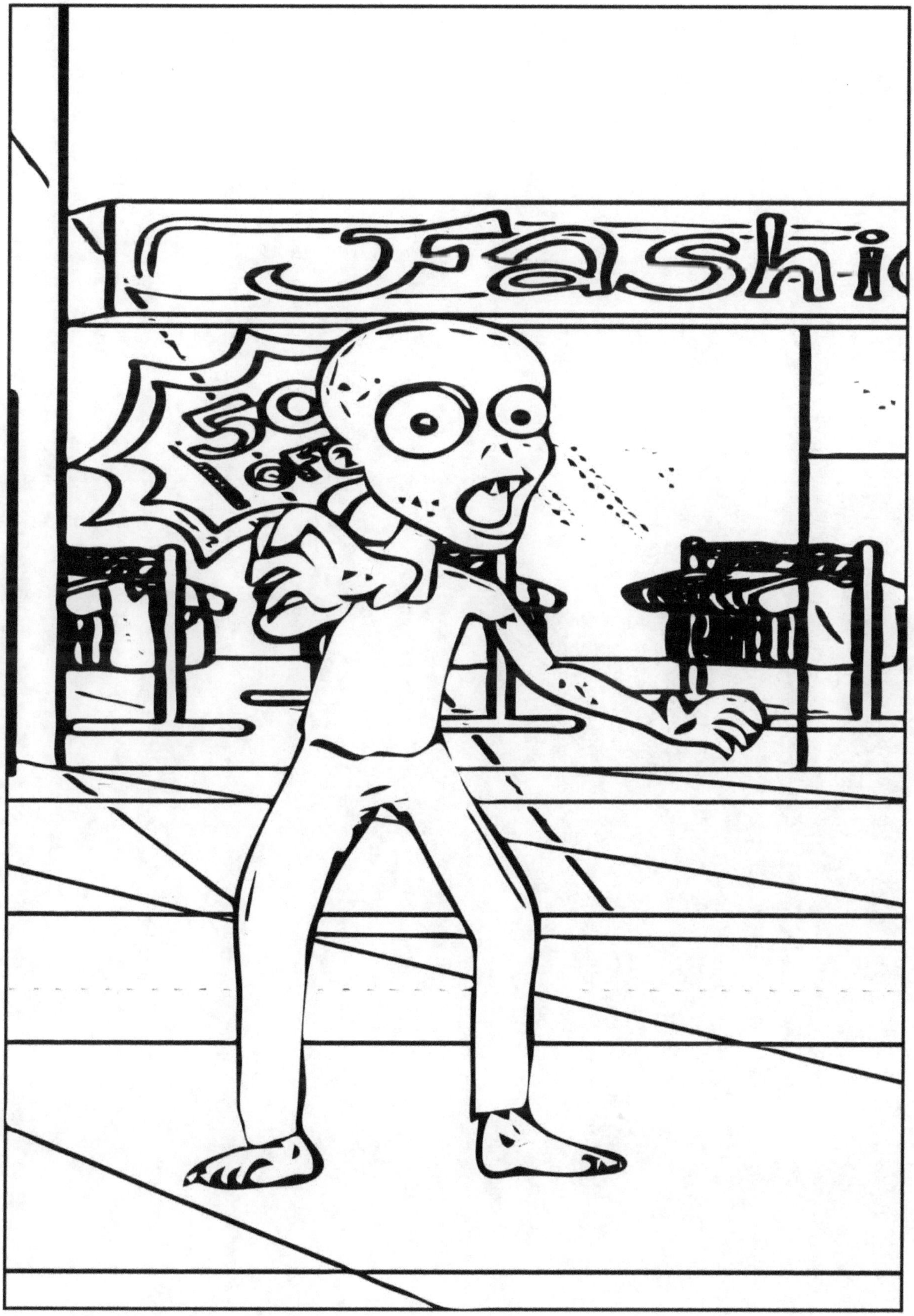
Fashi

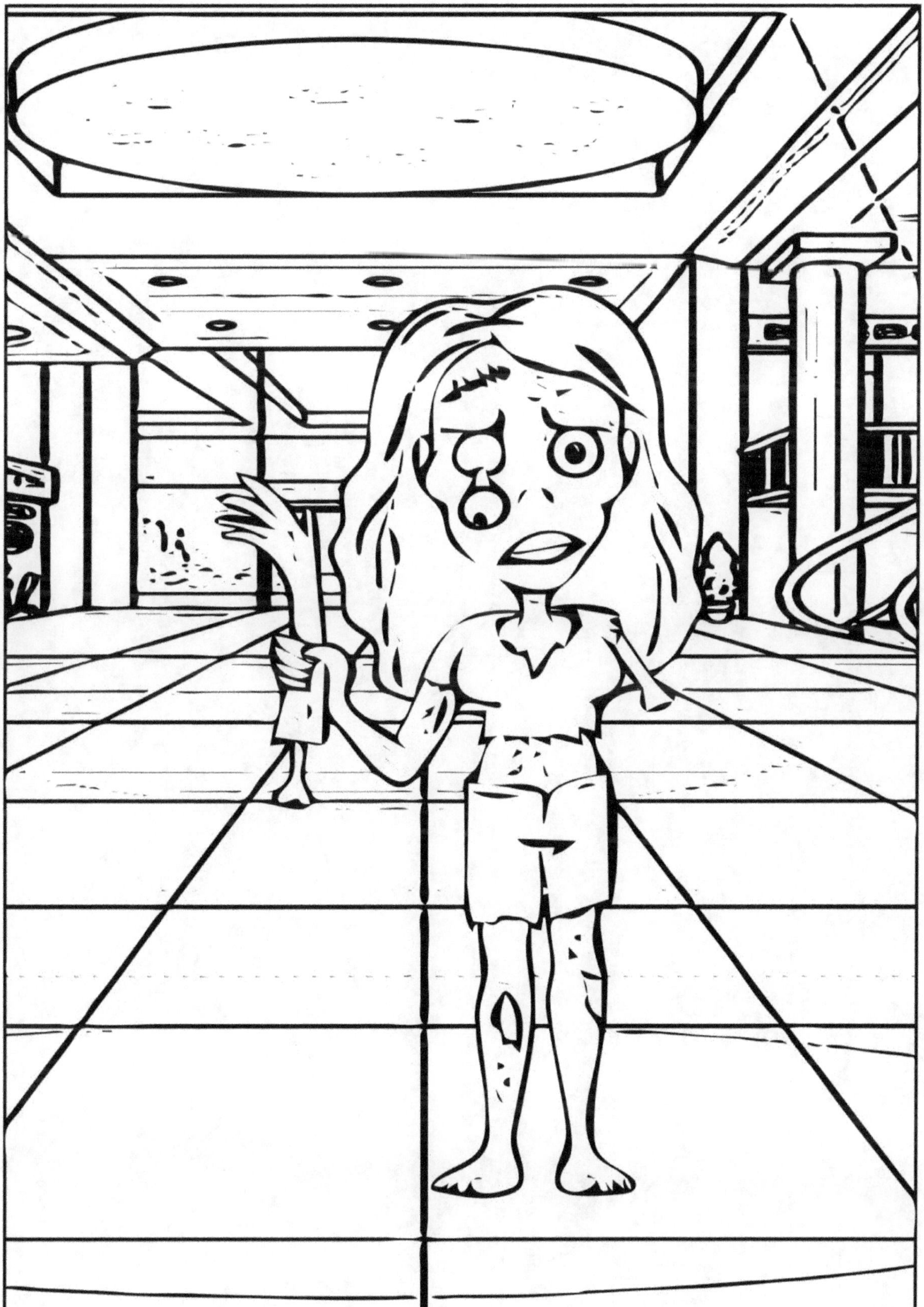

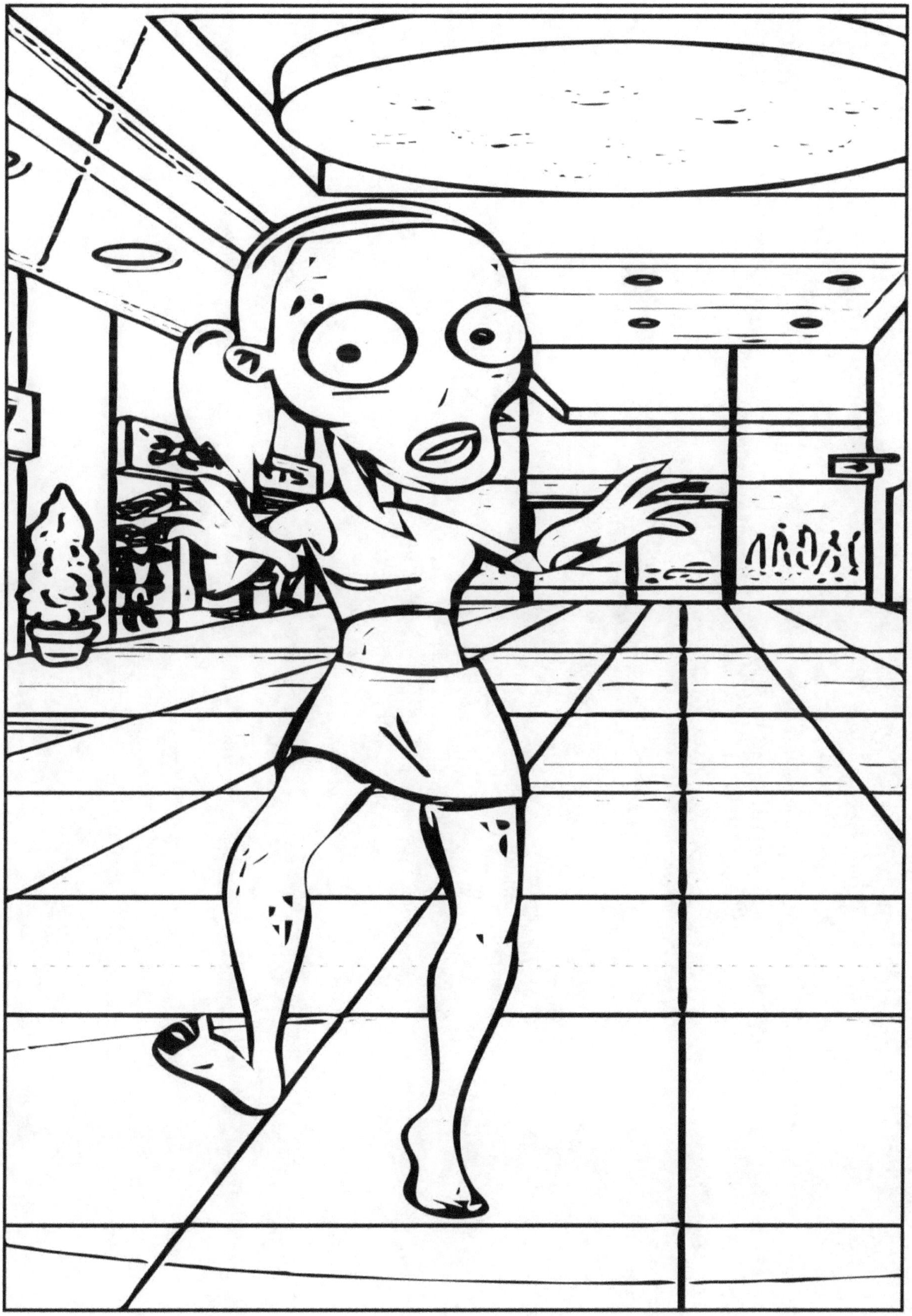

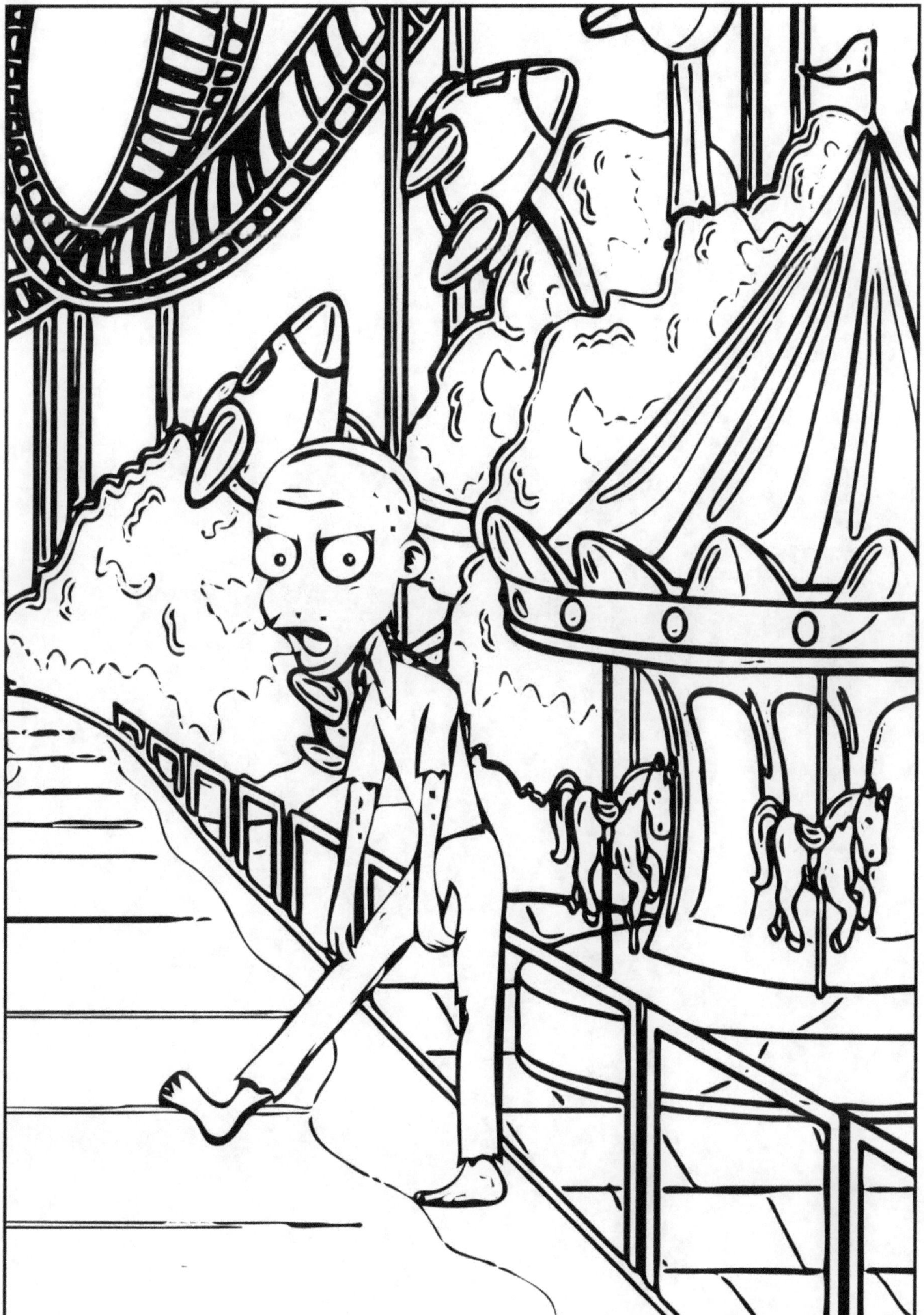

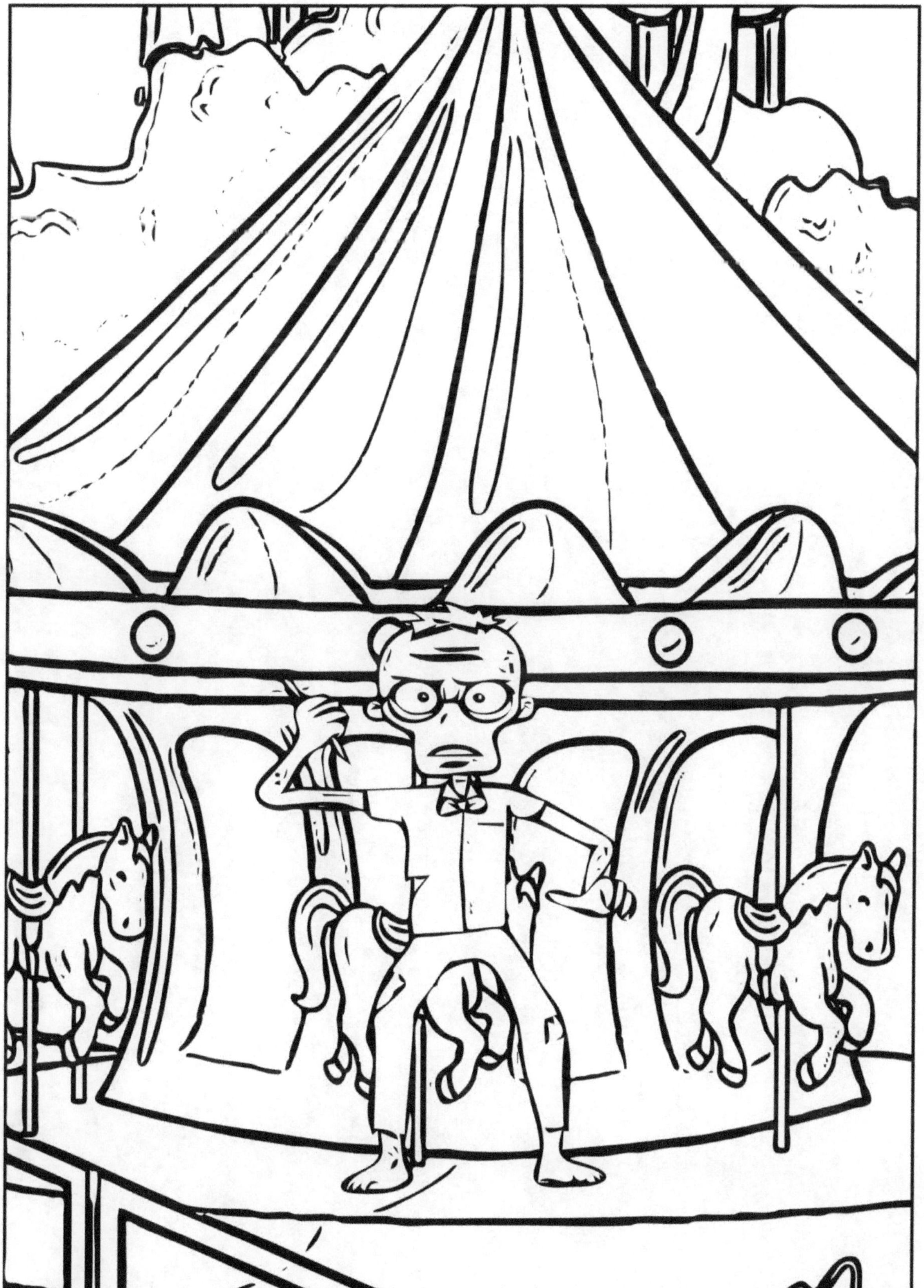

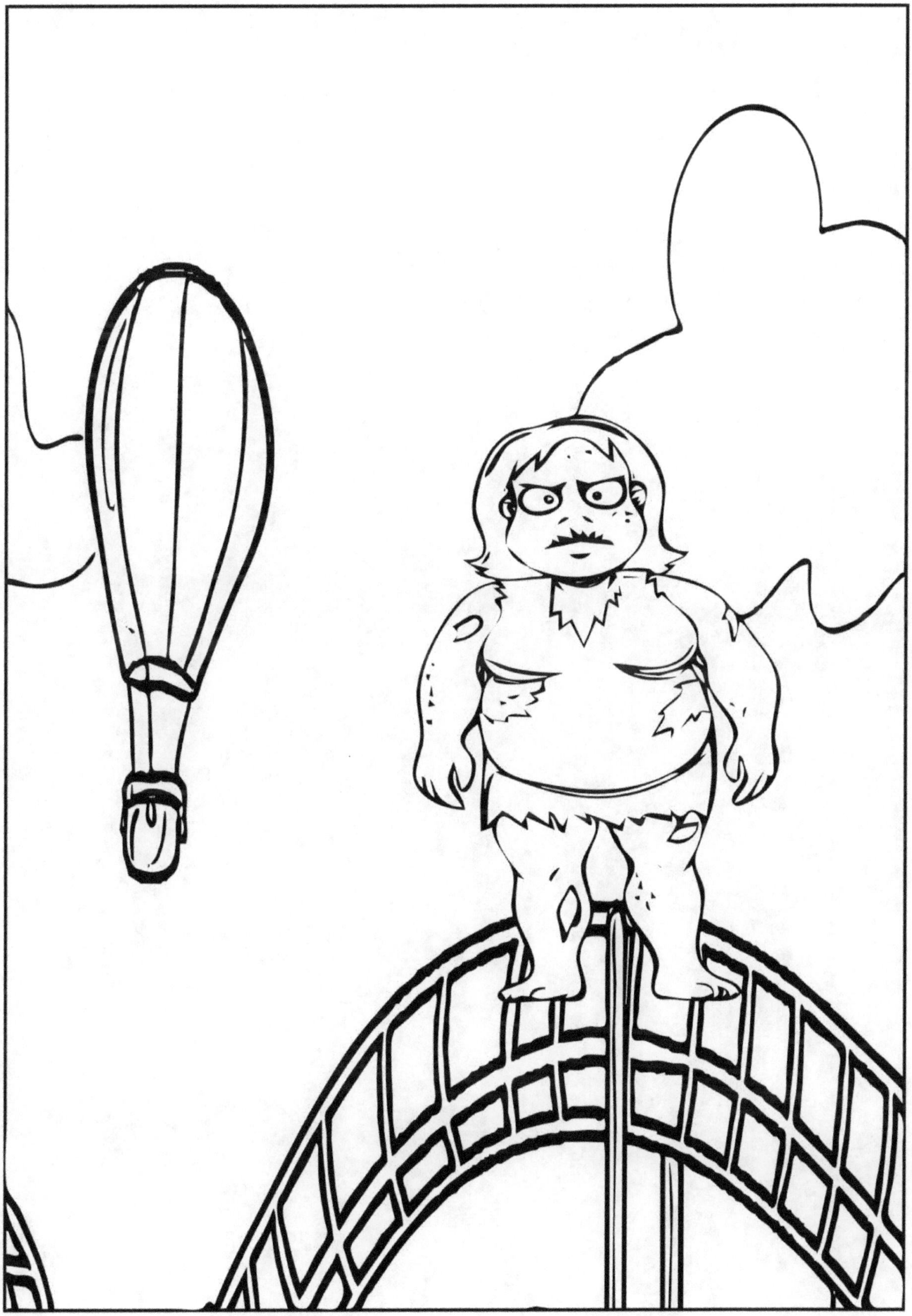

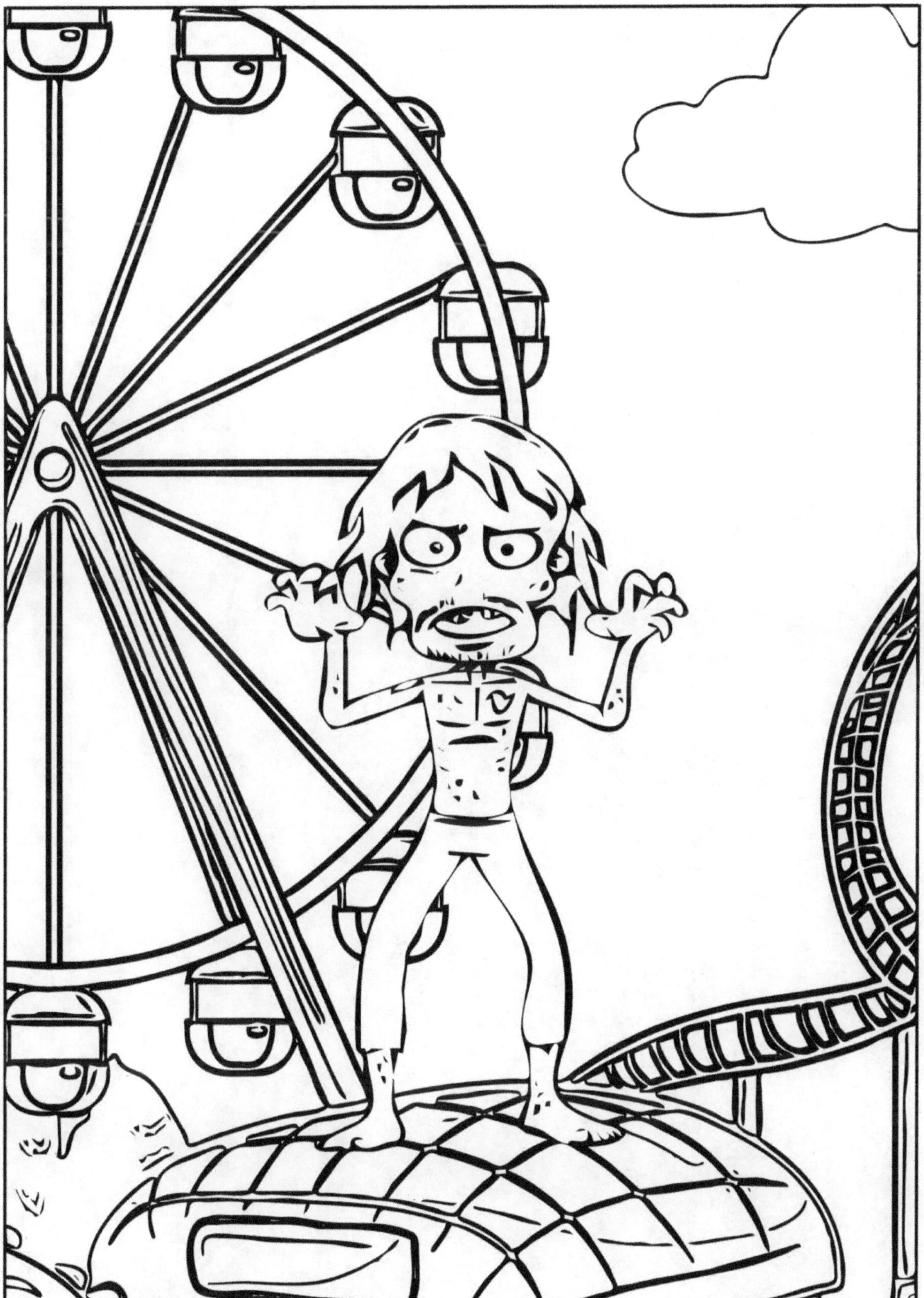

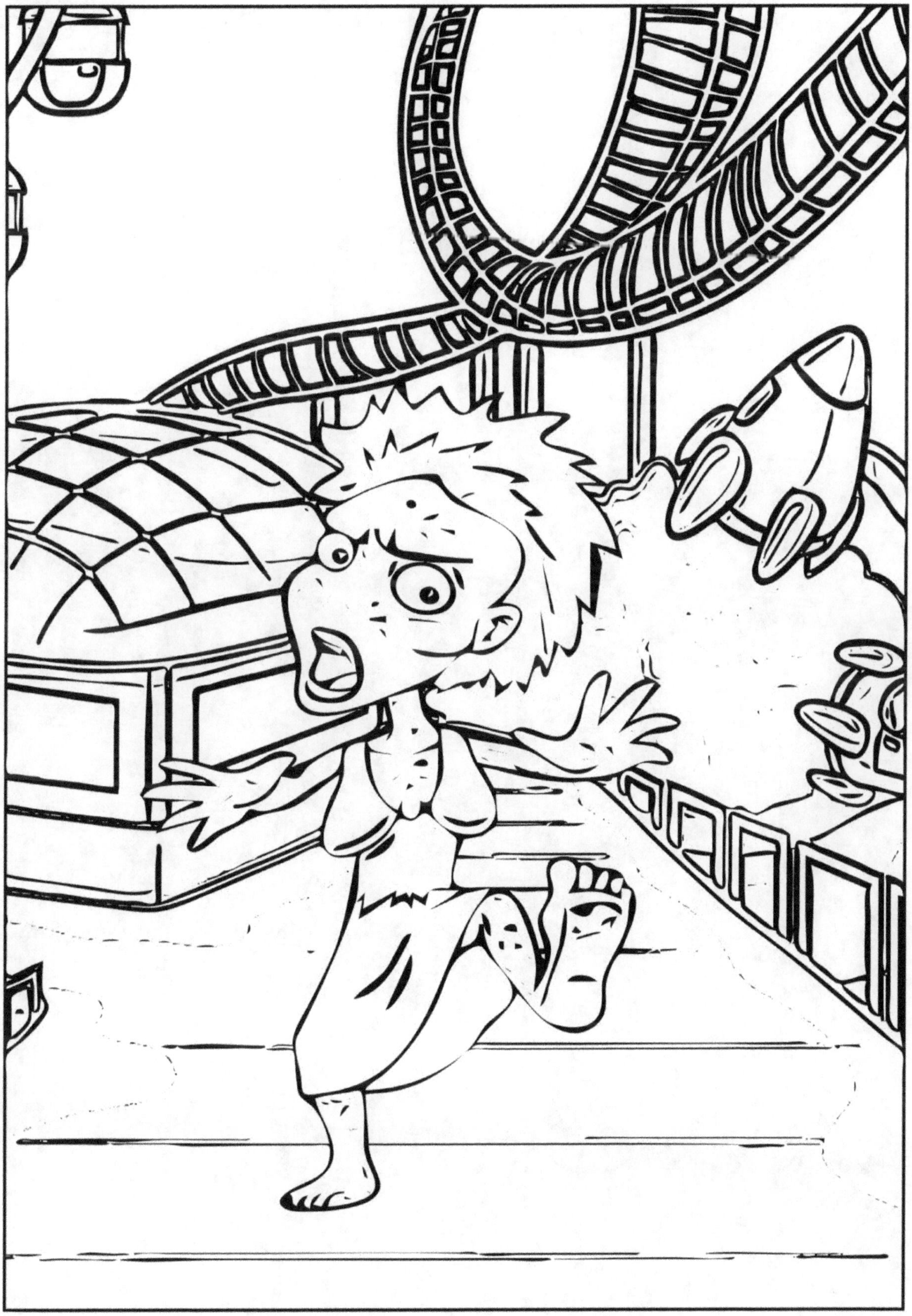

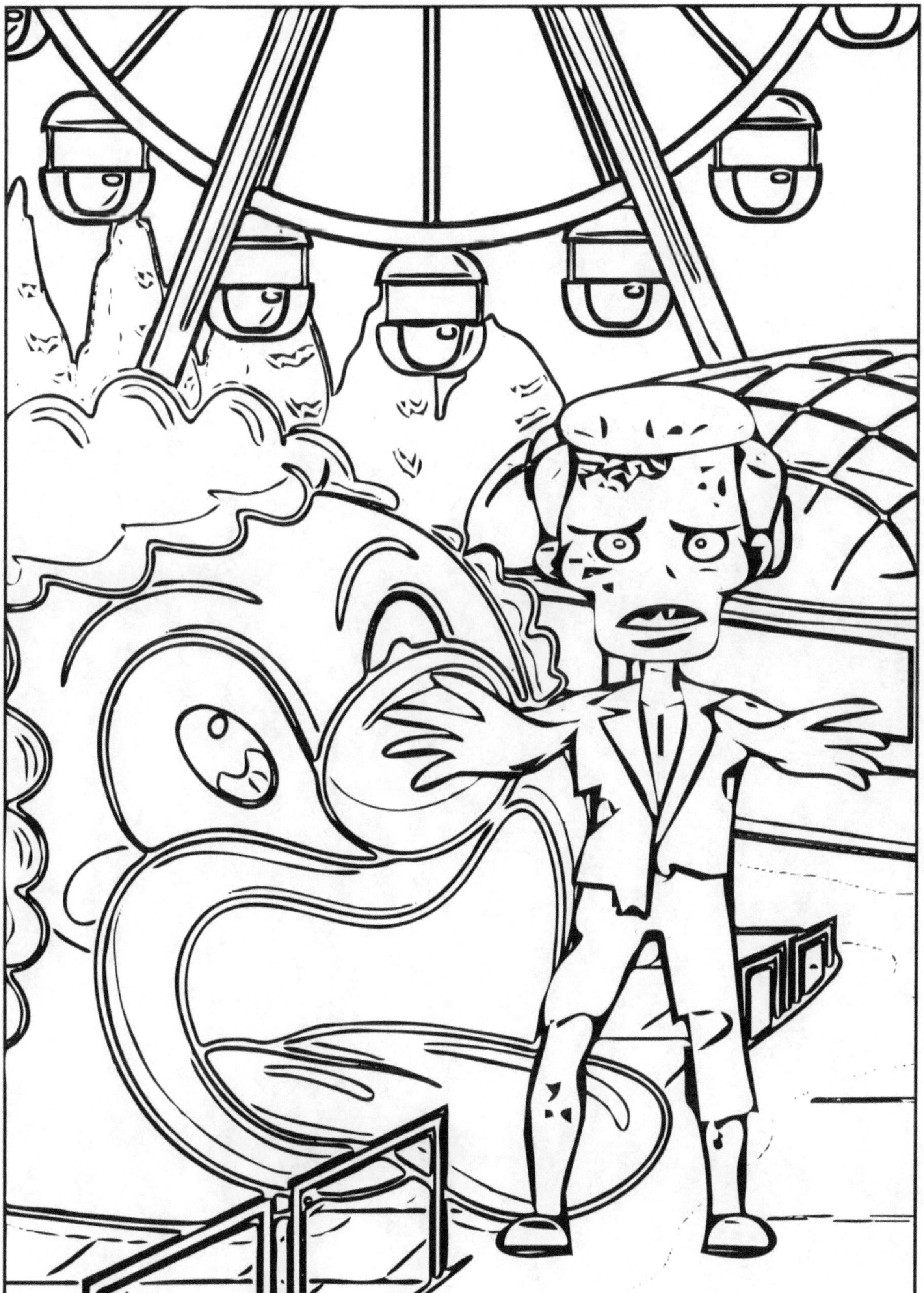

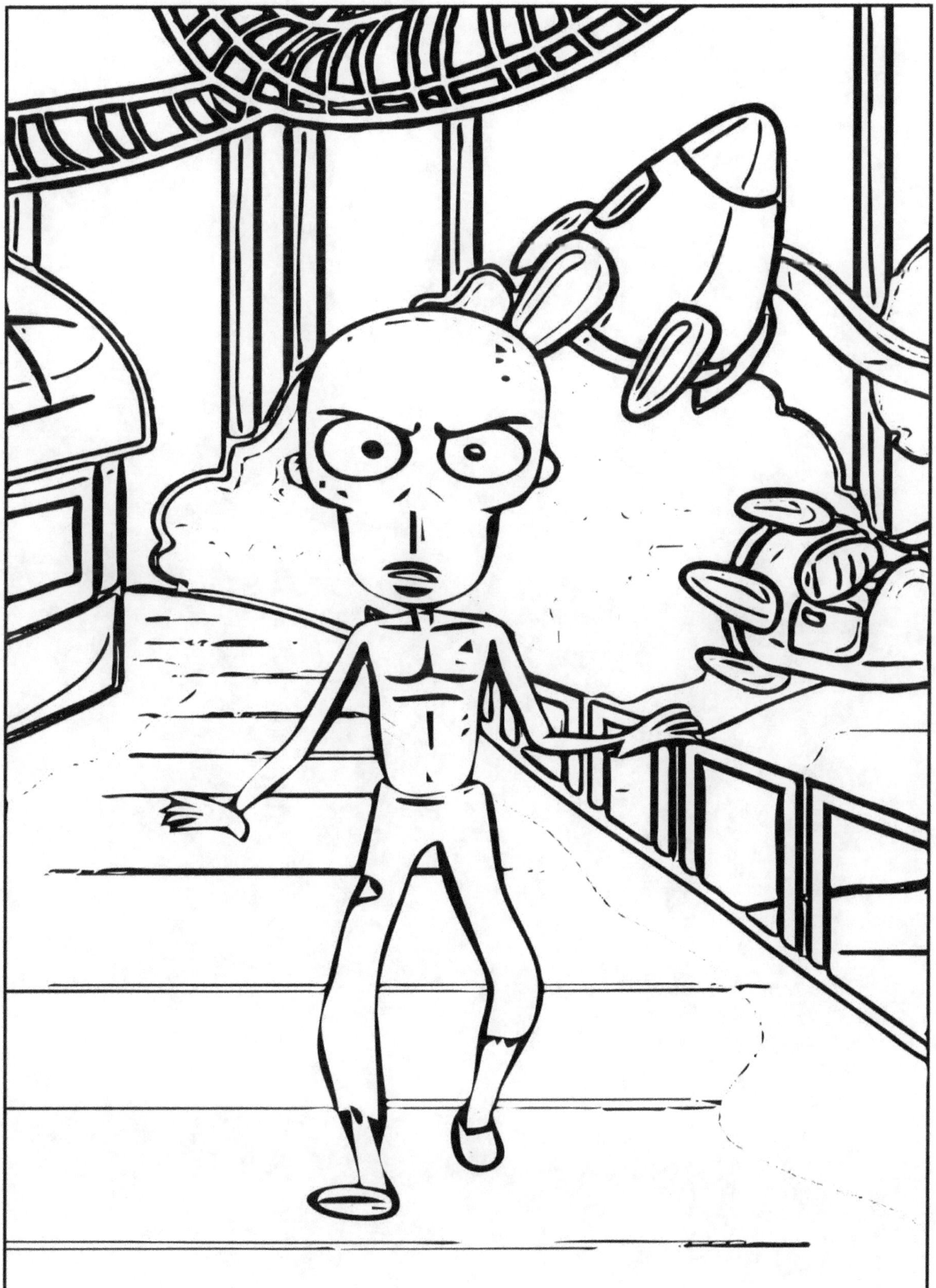

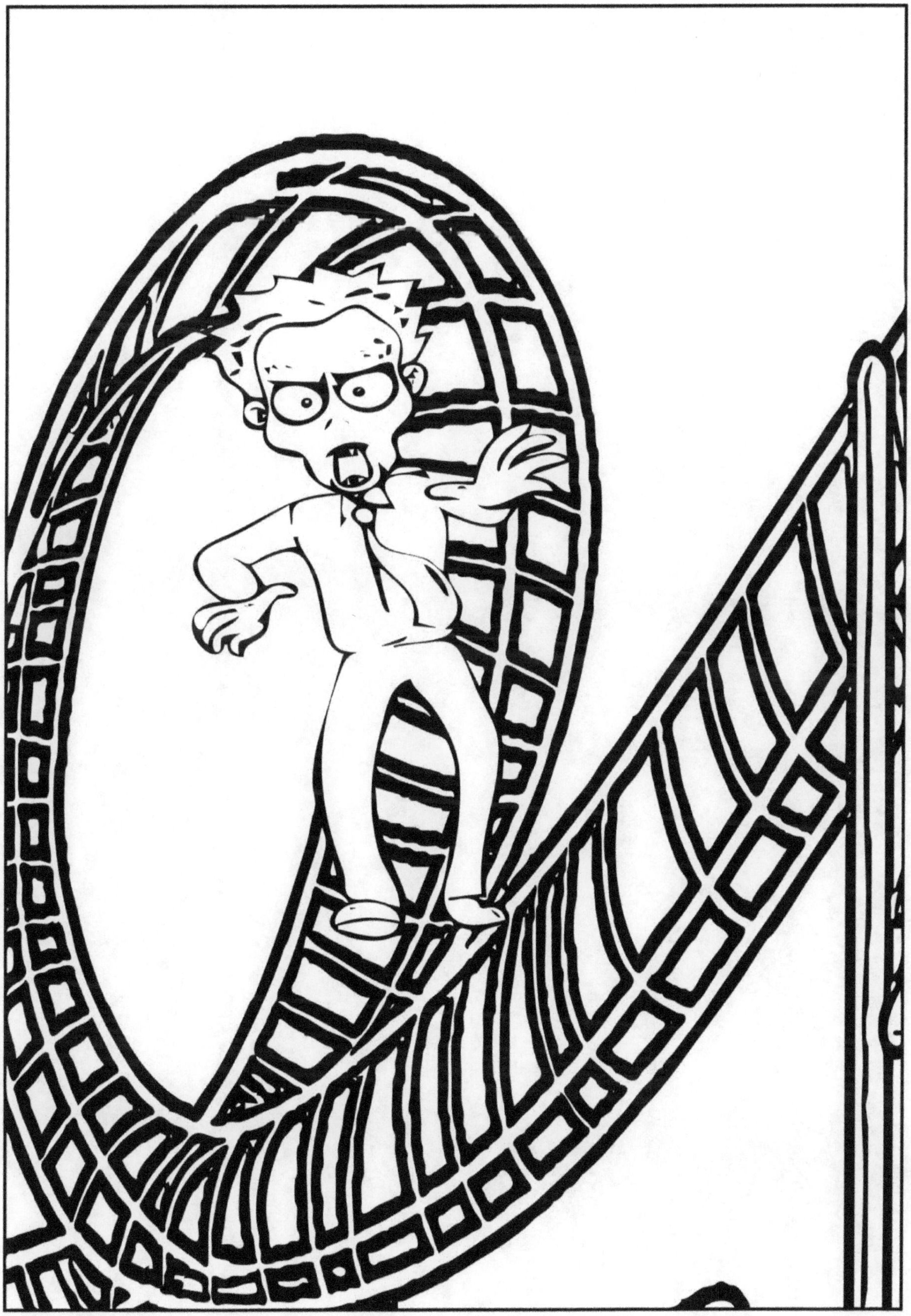

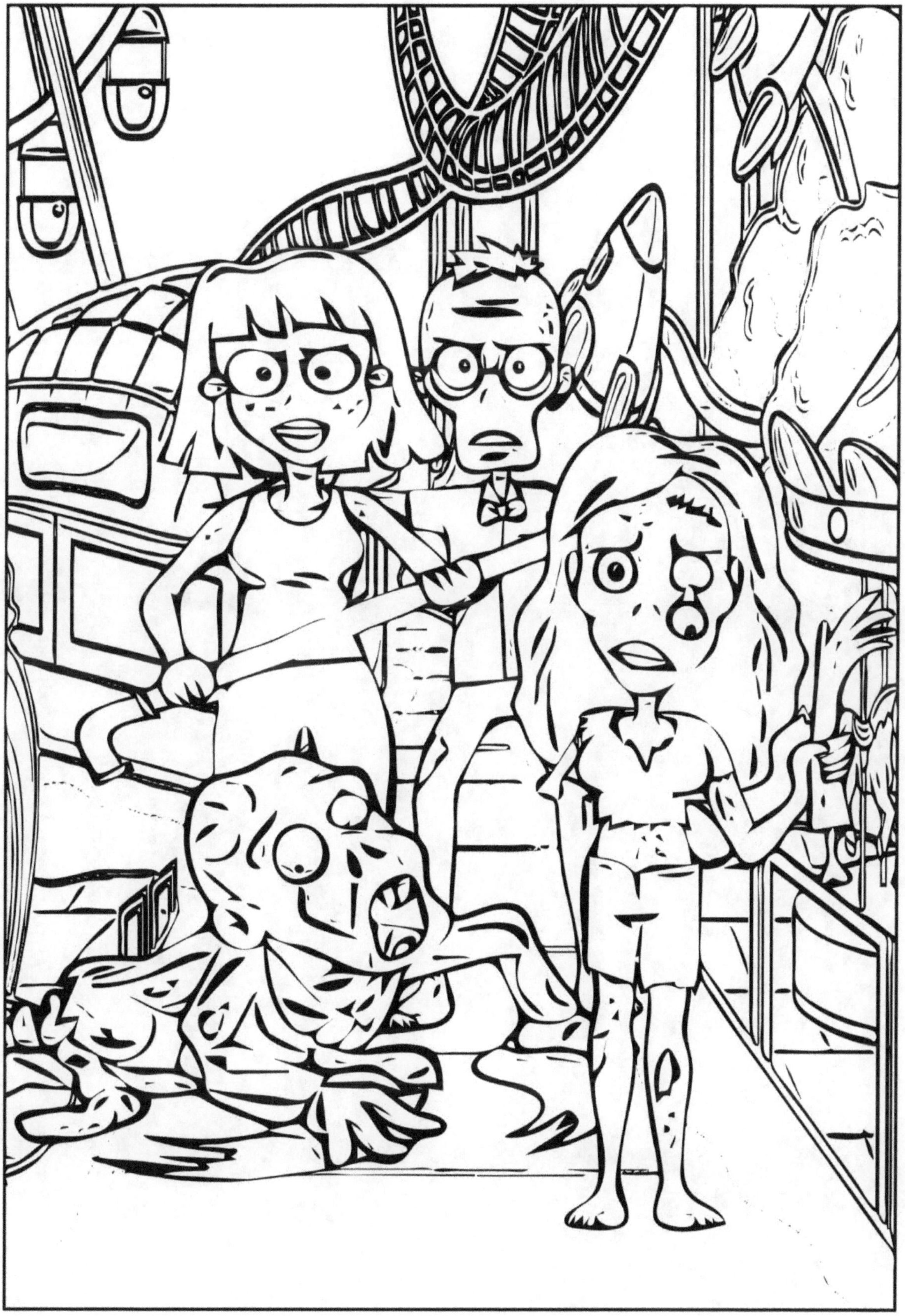

www.ingramcontent.com/pod-product-compliance
Lightning Source LLC
Chambersburg PA
CBHW080611180526
45168CB00007B/2867
* 9 7 8 1 5 1 7 3 7 8 5 8 5 *